Bill Gates

Founder of Microsoft

Greg Roza

PowerKiDS press.

New York

Published in 2017 by The Rosen Publishing Group, Inc.
29 East 21st Street, New York, NY 10010

First Edition

Editor: Caitlin McAneney
Book Design: Mickey Harmon

Photo Credits: Cover, pp. 1, 3–24, 26–32 (background) yxowert/Shutterstock.com; cover (Bill Gates), p. 29 Bloomberg/Contributor/Bloomberg/Getty Images; p. 5 Frederic Legrand - COMEO/Shutterstock.com; p. 7 Roy Stevens/Contributor/The LIFE Images Collection/Getty Images; pp. 9, 12, 13 Ron Wurzer/Stringer/Getty Images News/Getty Images; p. 11 Bill Johnson/Contributor/Denver Post/Getty Images; p. 15 https://en.wikipedia.org/wiki/Open_Letter_to_Hobbyists#/media/File:Bill_Gates_Letter_to_Hobbyists.jpg; p. 17 Michael Ochs Archives/Stringer/Moviepix/Getty Images; p. 18 adamico/Shutterstock.com; p. 19 Tommy Alven/Shutterstock.com; p. 21 Ann E. Yow-Dyson/Contributor/Archive Photos/Getty Images; p. 23 Doug Wilson/Contributor/The LIFE Images Collection/Getty Images; p. 25 RoSonic/Shutterstock.com; p. 27 https://en.wikipedia.org/wiki/Bill_Gates#/media/File:Bill_og_Melinda_Gates_2009-06-03_(bilde_01).JPG.

Library of Congress Cataloging-in-Publication Data

Roza, Greg, author.
 Bill Gates : founder of microsoft / Greg Roza.
     pages cm. — (Computer pioneers)
 Includes index.
 ISBN 978-1-5081-4828-9 (pbk.)
 ISBN 978-1-5081-4769-5 (6 pack)
 ISBN 978-1-5081-4820-3 (library binding)
 1. Gates, Bill, 1955—Juvenile literature. 2. Businessmen—United States—Biography—Juvenile literature. 3. Microsoft Corporation—History—Juvenile literature. 4. Computer software industry—United States—History—Juvenile literature. I. Title.
 HD9696.63.U62G37567 2016
 338.7'61004092—dc23
 [B]
                                    2015029433

Manufactured in the United States of America

CPSIA Compliance Information: Batch #BS16PK: For Further Information contact Rosen Publishing, New York, New York at 1-800-237-9932

Contents

King of Computers

You've likely heard the term "pioneer" before. You may think of Daniel Boone or Davy Crockett wearing a raccoon-skin hat, but a pioneer isn't necessarily someone who explored and settled in the American West. A computer pioneer is someone who's "broken new ground" and developed new ideas in the area of computer **technology**.

When talking about computer pioneers, many people today think of Bill Gates. Gates was a founder of Microsoft, and he's done a lot to shape modern computers. Gates has helped to make computer technology more **accessible** for all people. He's worked to promote the use of computer technology in libraries and schools. Today, Gates and his wife, Melinda, are **philanthropists** who help people around the world.

When Bill Gates was born in 1955, computers were huge machines that were mostly used by the military and universities. His work made them accessible to people who wanted to use them in their homes.

Young Genius

Growing up in Seattle, Washington, Gates showed an early interest in science and reading. He also loved to play games and sports with his family, and he was very competitive. These qualities helped Gates achieve success in business and **software** design.

As he got older, Gates became bored with school. He refused to do work, and he even talked back to his teachers. His parents thought Bill needed a challenge, so they enrolled him in a private school near Seattle named Lakeside. Two very important things happened to Gates in private school. The school had recently purchased an early kind of computer called a teleprinter, and Gates was instantly drawn to it. Gates also met Paul Allen, another student who became interested in the teleprinter.

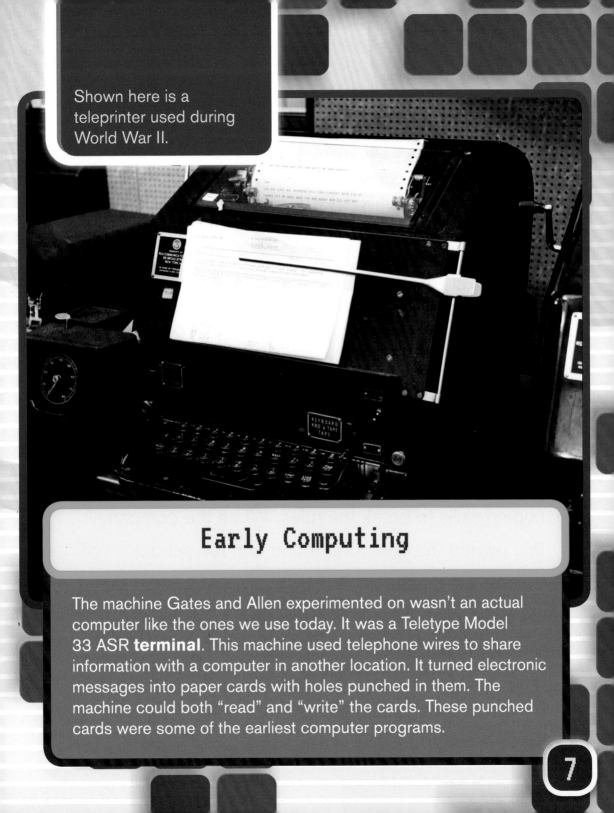

Shown here is a teleprinter used during World War II.

Early Computing

The machine Gates and Allen experimented on wasn't an actual computer like the ones we use today. It was a Teletype Model 33 ASR **terminal**. This machine used telephone wires to share information with a computer in another location. It turned electronic messages into paper cards with holes punched in them. The machine could both "read" and "write" the cards. These punched cards were some of the earliest computer programs.

Troublemakers

Gates and Allen quickly learned two **programming languages** called BASIC and FORTRAN. When he was just 13, Gates wrote the code for his first program: a tic-tac-toe game against the computer.

The two computer pioneers were constantly in the computer lab. The school had to pay another company for time on the computer, but Gates and Allen soon found a way to get free time by "hacking" the company's computer. That means they used coding skills to break the rules. When the company that owned the computer found out, the school banned Gates and Allen from the lab. However, the clever boys found a way to get their rights back. In exchange, they fixed the glitches, or errors, in the company's software that allowed them to get free time.

Paul Allen

Bill Gates

Gates and Allen sold their first computer program to the City of Seattle in 1970. The "Traf-O-Data" was a traffic-tracking program, and they made $20,000 from it!

The Lie That Started Microsoft

Gates graduated from Lakeside in 1973 and enrolled in Harvard University. His parents wanted him to become a lawyer, but once again, Gates was drawn to the computer lab. His old friend, Paul Allen, moved to Boston for a job as a programmer. Allen got Gates a job with the company, too.

In 1974, Gates and Allen read an article about the Altair 8800 computer kit. This kit allowed people to build, modify, and program their own "microcomputer." On a whim, Gates called the Altair's creators to tell them he'd created BASIC software that would run on the new machine. This was a lie! However, the company was very interested and asked to see the program. Gates and Allen rushed to the Harvard computer lab and got to work.

The Boston company that Allen and Gates worked for was called Honeywell. This company developed some of the earliest business computers. Honeywell also made computer components, or parts, for the Apollo space missions that landed men on the moon.

Call the Interpreter

Allen and Gates realized very quickly that the Altair 8800 would be useless without software. They created Altair BASIC for the microcomputer, which is a BASIC interpreter. An interpreter is a program that performs instructions written in computer language.

After several months of hard work, Gates and Allen had a program to show the Altair 8800's makers—a company named Micro Instrumentation and **Telemetry** Systems (MITS). However, they still had no idea if it would work. They didn't even have an Altair computer to experiment with! With their fingers crossed, the computing duo traveled to the MITS office in Albuquerque, New Mexico. The program worked perfectly, and the company liked it so much they hired Gates and Allen to create more software for them.

Altair 8800

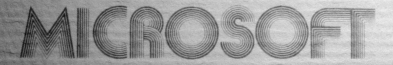

MICROSOFT

William H. Gates
President

819 Two Park Central Tower, Albuquerque, NM 87108
(505) 256-3600

The name "Microsoft" is a combination of "microcomputer" and "software."

Gates's initial success prompted him to drop out of Harvard and pursue programming full-time. He and Allen called their new business venture "Micro-Soft." In 1976, they registered the Microsoft **trademark**. Soon after, they began creating programs for other companies.

The Open Letter

More people started buying the Altair 8800 and other early microcomputers, but few people were buying the Altair BASIC software. The people who bought the Altair 8800 were hobbyists. They often made copies of software and shared it with other hobbyists. Today, this is called software piracy. Others have pointed out that sharing software helped speed up the growing microcomputer revolution.

In February 1976, Gates wrote an "Open Letter to Hobbyists," which appeared in the Homebrew Computer Club's newsletter. This club's members included several notable computer pioneers, including Steve Jobs and Stephen Wozniak. Gates explained that stealing software would "prevent good software from being written," since programmers worked many hours and got paid so little. Gates's letter upset some people, but he firmly believed programmers had a right to protect their work.

In his letter, Gates estimated that with the poor sales and all the hours they spent developing the software, they'd made just $2 an hour. "Is this fair?" Gates asked. Software piracy is still a highly debated topic today.

-2-
February 3, 1976

An Open Letter to Hobbyists

To me, the most critical thing in the hobby market right now is the lack of good software courses, books and software itself. Without good software and an owner who understands programming, a hobby computer is wasted. Will quality software be written for the hobby market?

Almost a year ago, Paul Allen and myself, expecting the hobby market to expand, hired Monte Davidoff and developed Altair BASIC. Though the initial work took only two months, the three of us have spent most of the last year documenting, improving and adding features to BASIC. Now we have 4K, 8K, EXTENDED, ROM and DISK BASIC. The value of the computer time we have used exceeds $40,000.

The feedback we have gotten from the hundreds of people who say they are using BASIC has all been positive. Two surprising things are apparent, however. 1) Most of these "users" never bought BASIC (less than 10% of all Altair owners have bought BASIC), and 2) The amount of royalties we have received from sales to hobbyists makes the time spent on Altair BASIC worth less than $2 an hour.

Why is this? As the majority of hobbyists must be aware, most of you steal your software. Hardware must be paid for, but software is something to share. Who cares if the people who worked on it get paid?

Is this fair? One thing you don't do by stealing software is get back at MITS for some problem you may have had. MITS doesn't make money selling software. The royalty paid to us, the manual, the tape and the overhead make it a break-even operation. One thing you do is prevent good software from being written. Who can afford to do professional work for nothing? What hobbyist can put 3-man years into programming, finding all bugs, documenting his product and distribute for free? The fact is, no one besides us has invested a lot of money in hobby software. We have written 6800 BASIC, and are writing 8080 APL and 6800 APL, but there is very little incentive to make this software available to hobbyists. Most directly, the thing you do is theft.

What about the guys who re-sell Altair BASIC, aren't they making money on hobby software? Yes, but those who have been reported to us may lose in the end. They are the ones who give hobbyists a bad name, and should be kicked out of any club meeting they show up at.

I would appreciate letters from any one who wants to pay up, or has a suggestion or comment. Just write me at 1180 Alvarado SE, #114, Albuquerque, New Mexico, 87108. Nothing would please me more than being able to hire ten programmers and deluge the hobby market with good software.

Bill Gates
Bill Gates
General Partner, Micro-Soft

Second and Final

When members of the Homebrew Computer Club read Gates's letter in the club's February 1976 newsletter, many of them responded directly to Gates. In the club's April 1976 newsletter, Gates wrote "A Second and Final Letter" to clarify his original statements. He said that hobbyists should make and share programs that are less complex, since people will need programs to run on new microcomputers. However, software companies that make complex software, such as interpreters, require a return on investment to make it worthwhile.

Success!

Despite the initial problems Gates and Allen faced, the newly formed Microsoft quickly recovered. They began writing BASIC software that would work on personal computers, or PCs. They **licensed** software to Apple Computers, Radio Shack, Texas Instruments, and other computer manufacturers.

Thanks to Gates's competitive nature and strong business skills, Microsoft became a huge success. In 1978, Gates moved Microsoft to Bellevue, Washington. The company now had 25 employees. That year, when Bill Gates was just 23 years old, Microsoft earned $2.5 million.

In 1980, the computer company IBM approached Microsoft to create software that could operate a new personal computer it was ready to release. The licensing deal Gates developed for IBM proved to be a groundbreaking and profitable one for Microsoft.

Though Bill Gates was still very young, he found great success through Microsoft and made very smart business decisions.

17

IBM released the IBM PC in 1980. The company hired Microsoft to develop an **operating system** (OS) for it. Gates and his team of programmers created Microsoft Disk Operating System, or MS-DOS. However, they didn't do it from scratch. Gates purchased software from another company and used it as the framework for a new operating system for the IBM PC.

Microsoft paid $50,000 for all rights to the software MS-DOS was based on, so the company officially owned it. This brilliant business move allowed Microsoft to license the software to other computer companies as well. Microsoft exploded! By 1983, Microsoft had offices in Great Britain and Japan. Soon, Microsoft software was run on an estimated 30 percent of the world's computers.

Microsoft's MS-DOS was originally released on 3.5-inch floppy disks.

Commands and Graphics

MS-DOS is a command-line **interface**. That means users need to type in lines of instructions in order to communicate with the computer. MS-DOS was last updated in 1994, although a version of it is still used. MS-DOS was replaced by newer operating systems—such as Windows and Mac OS—which use **graphical** elements that allow users to communicate with the computer. These operating systems feature a graphical user interface, or GUI (GOO-ee).

The GUI Revolution

In the early 1980s, Microsoft briefly helped develop software for Apple Computers, and the two companies shared information. This collaboration showed Gates and Allen the need for a graphical user interface to make computers easier to use for the average person. In early 1984, Apple released its first GUI operating system, simply called System. About two years later, Microsoft released Windows OS. Windows was not an instant success. It took a few years for Microsoft to perfect it.

The change from MS-DOS to Windows allowed average people to better understand and use computers. Instead of typing commands, users now used a mouse, visual icons, movable windows, drop-down menus, and many other conveniences. Since the earliest version, Windows operating systems have been hugely popular all over the world.

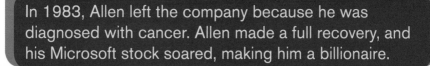

In 1983, Allen left the company because he was diagnosed with cancer. Allen made a full recovery, and his Microsoft stock soared, making him a billionaire.

ALLEN

Microsoft vs. Apple

For years, computer fans have argued about who first developed a GUI for home computers. Apple released System about two years before Microsoft released Windows. Many people complained that Gates stole the idea from Steve Jobs, co-founder of Apple Computers. However, many people don't know that the two computer pioneers shared company information in the early 1980s, which surely led to benefits for both Apple and Microsoft.

Software Giant

The personal computer market took off, and Gates was set to be the king of computer software. Thanks to the success of Windows and other Microsoft software, Gates became a millionaire in 1986 when he was 31. He became the youngest billionaire ever just one year later in 1987! Microsoft's success continued to grow in the early 1990s as Gates and his team improved Windows OS. In 1995, Gates became the richest man in the world.

Even though Microsoft was a worldwide success, Gates still worked hard to develop new software. He continued to revolutionize the personal computer market with powerful new software, such as Microsoft Office, which remains the most popular group of business tools in the world today.

In this photograph from 1987, Gates holds up a copy of Microsoft Bookshelf on CD-ROM, which was a new technology at the time. One CD could hold thousands of pages of reference material.

Microsoft Bookshelf
Special Preview Edition
Microsoft
ZIP Code and Post Office Directory
94102
20856
ROGET'S
The Chicago Manual of Style
Daniells Business Information

Exploring the Internet

Before there was an Internet there was ARPAnet, which was an early computer network that linked two universities in California in 1969. In 1971, a computer system at the University of Hawaii was connected to the network, and ARPAnet grew quickly from there, becoming the foundation of the Internet. It wasn't until 1991 that computer pioneer Tim Berners-Lee created the World Wide Web, which is a way of accessing information on the Internet.

As the World Wide Web took shape, Gates knew he needed to create software to compete with other computer companies. In 1995, Microsoft released Internet Explorer, which was a very popular **web browser** for many years. Internet Explorer allowed people all over the world to "surf the web" for information, friends, entertainment, and much more.

In July 2015, Microsoft released Windows 10, which includes the browser Microsoft Edge (originally called Project Spartan). This is a faster, simpler version of Internet Explorer.

Microsoft in Court

During the 1990s, Microsoft and Gates were the focus of investigations and court cases. The U.S. government sued Microsoft on the basis that the company was **monopolizing** the computer software industry. Again, Gates had to defend his use of licensing to protect his software creations. In the end, Microsoft lost the case and had to divide into two separate companies: one to make Windows OS and one to make other software. Still, Gates continued to defend his right to license his products.

From Computer Genius to Philanthropist

Gates met his future wife, Melinda, while she was working as a product manager for Microsoft. Melinda helped develop several key programs for Microsoft, including the digital encyclopedia Encarta. Bill and Melinda married in 1994. They have three children.

In 2000, Gates stepped down as CEO of Microsoft and became the chief software architect. That means he was in charge of the team designing new software. That same year, Bill and Melinda combined several charitable organizations they'd founded to form the Bill and Melinda Gates Foundation. In 2008, Gates stepped down from full-time work at Microsoft in order to focus on charitable efforts. Since then, Bill and Melinda have devoted their time, money, and talents to making life better for people all over the world.

Bill and Melinda have become two of the greatest philanthropists in the world.

The Bill and Melinda Gates Foundation is helping improve worldwide health and the treatment of diseases. Some of their many charitable contributions may affect you as you go to school. The College-Ready Education and Postsecondary Success programs are designed to prepare U.S. students for success in college. The Gates Foundation has also worked to improve computer technology in American schools.

Some people have said Bill Gates isn't really an inventor and doesn't deserve all the credit he gets for being a computer pioneer. But it's clear to see that Gates's contributions to the computer revolution are numerous, including developing advanced software for average computer users in an era when few people knew how to create it.

Through his dedication to charity, Bill Gates shows how much he cares about those who are less fortunate than he is. He's not only made huge contributions to the computer world, but he's made huge contributions to those in need as well.

STRENGTHENING GLOBAL FOOD SECURITY

Timeline

October 28, 1955
William Henry Gates III is born.

1967
Bill Gates goes to Lakeside School. He meets Paul Allen and discovers computers.

1973
Gates enrolls in Harvard University.

1974
Gates and Allen create Altair BASIC. Soon after, they form Micro-soft, renamed Microsoft.

1976
Gates writes an "Open Letter to Hobbyists."

1980
Microsoft releases MS-DOS and licenses it to several computer companies.

1985
Microsoft releases Windows OS.

1987
Gates becomes the youngest billionaire ever.

1994
Bill Gates marries Melinda Ann French.

1995
MIcrosoft releases Internet Explorer.

2000
Gates steps down as CEO of Microsoft to become the chief software architect.

2000
Bill and Melinda Gates Foundation is founded.

2015
Microsoft releases the browser Edge.

Glossary

accessible: Easy to use or understand.

graphical: Having to do with pictures and shapes, also called graphics.

interface: The connection between two things that are communicating, such as a person and a computer.

license: To give or sell official permission to a person or company to do or use something.

monopolize: To obtain exclusive control of a trade, service, or product.

operating system: The software that controls a computer's main functions.

philanthropist: Someone who promotes the health and welfare of others, especially through donations of money to good causes.

programming language: A language designed to give instructions to a computer.

software: Programs used by a computer.

technology: The way people do something using tools and the tools that they use.

telemetry: A process by which information is collected in one place and viewed in another using computers.

terminal: A computer or display connected to a computer system that is used for receiving and viewing information.

trademark: A word or image legally associated with a person or company, which cannot be used by other companies.

web browser: A computer program that allows users to search the World Wide Web.

Index

Websites

Due to the changing nature of Internet links, PowerKids Press has developed an online list of websites related to the subject of this book. This site is updated regularly. Please use this link to access the list: www.powerkidslinks.com/compio/gates